John Kember and Peter Bowman

Recorder Sight-Reading 1

Déchiffrage pour la flûte à bec 1
Vom-Blatt-Spiel auf der Blockflöte 1

A fresh approach / Nouvelle approche
Eine erfrischend neue Methode

ED 12957
ISMN M-2201-2570-6
ISBN 978-1-902455-80-8

www.schott-music.com

Mainz · London · Madrid · New York · Paris · Prague · Tokyo · Toronto
© 2007 SCHOTT MUSIC Ltd, London · Printed in Germany

ED 12957

British Library Cataloguing-in-Publication Data.
A catalogue record for this book is available from the British Library
ISMN M-2201-2570-6
ISBN 978-1-902455-80-8

© 2007 Schott Music Ltd, London.

All rights reserved. No part of this publication may be reproduced, stored in
a retrieval system, or transmitted, in any form or by any means, electronic, mechanical,
photocopying, recording or otherwise, without prior written permission from
Schott Music Ltd, 48 Great Marlborough Street, London W1F 7BB

French translation: Agnès Ausseur
German translation: Ute Corleis
Cover design by www.adamhaystudio.com
Music setting and page layout by Peter Nickol
Printed in Germany S&Co.8214

Contents
Sommaire/Inhalt

Preface

Recorder Sight-Reading 1 aims to establish good practice and provide an early introduction to the essential skill of sight-reading.

Sight-reading needs to be set regularly but is of little value unless the pieces sight-read are subsequently played to the teacher. Ideally, sight-reading in some form should become a regular part of a student's routine each time they play the recorder.

This book aims to establish the habit early in a student's recorder playing. Of course, names of notes and time values need to be thoroughly known and understood, but equally sight-reading is helped by awareness of shape and direction.

There are seven sections in this book, each of which introduces new notes, rhythms, articulations, dynamics and Italian terms in a logical sequence, much as you would find in a beginner's recorder tutor. The emphasis is on providing idiomatic tunes and structures rather than sterile sight-reading exercises. Each section begins with several solo examples and concludes with duets and accompanied pieces, enabling the player to gain experience of sight-reading within the context of ensemble playing.

Sections 1–5 employ the soprano (descant) recorder only. The alto (treble) recorder is introduced in Section 6.

Section 1 uses the notes G – B, together with simple rhythms and time signatures. Melodic material emphasises movement by step, simple phrase structures, repeated notes and repeated melodic shapes (sequences).

Section 2 introduces the notes C and D and 3/4 time. Movement by skip is added and some slurs are suggested.

Section 3 introduces low F♯ and upper C♯ together with the key and key signature of D major. The interval of a 4th occurs as do some slurred quavers (eighth notes), and the dotted-crotchet/quaver figure (♩. ♪). The concept of dynamics is introduced, interpreting *f* as 'strong' and *p* as 'gentle'.

Section 4 extends the range from low E and D to high E. The time signature of 3/8 is introduced leading to the use of 6/8 time. Semiquavers (sixteenth notes) occur in pairs in 3/8 time and the interval of a 5th is introduced.

Section 5 extends the range further, from low C to high F♯, and adds the key of D minor. Familiar time values and time signatures are used with the addition of examples in 5/4 time. Trills are used in both long and short form.

Section 6 adds the notes B♭, E♭ and A♭. The keys of F and B♭ major, and of C, E, G (in the alto) and A minor are introduced, as is the interval of a 6th. The mordent is added to the ornaments already used and use is made of short chromatic phrases. The alto recorder is first introduced.

Section 7 introduces high G, and the keys of E♭, E (alto) and A major. Extended chromatic phrases, the inverted mordent and some simple syncopations are included.

To the pupil: why sight-reading?

When you are faced with a new piece and asked to play it, whether at home, in a lesson or in an exam or audition, there is no one there to help you – except yourself! Sight-reading tests your ability to read the time and notes correctly and to observe the phrasing and dynamics quickly.

The aim of this book is to help you to teach yourself. The book gives guidance on what to look for and how best to prepare in a very short time by observing the time and key signatures, the shape of the melody and the marks of expression. These short pieces progress gradually to help you to build up your confidence and observation, and enable you to sight-read accurately. At the end of each section there are duets to play with your teacher or friends and pieces with piano accompaniment, which will test your ability to sight-read while something else is going on. This is a necessary skill when playing with a recorder consort, orchestra or other ensemble.

If you sight-read something every time you play your recorder you will be amazed how much better you will become. Remember, if you can sight-read most of the tunes you are asked to learn you will be able to concentrate on the 'tricky bits' and complete them quickly.

Think of the tunes in this book as 'mini-pieces' and try to learn them quickly and correctly. Then when you are faced with real sight-reading you will be well equipped to succeed on a first attempt.

You are on your own now!

Préface

Le propos de ce premier volume de déchiffrage pour la flûte à bec est de fournir une initiation et un entraînement solide aux principes de la lecture à vue.

La lecture à vue doit être pratiquée régulièrement et son action sera encore accrue si les pièces déchiffrées sont ensuite jouées au professeur. L'idéal serait que le déchiffrage prenne régulièrement place dans la routine de travail de l'élève à chaque fois qu'il prend sa flûte à bec.

L'objectif est ici d'établir l'habitude de la lecture à vue très tôt dans l'étude de la flûte à bec. Le déchiffrage suppose, bien sûr, que les noms et les valeurs de notes soient complètement assimilés et compris mais il s'appuie également sur la reconnaissance des contours et de la direction mélodiques.

Ce volume comporte sept parties dont chacune correspond à l'introduction de notes, de rythmes, de phrasés, de nuances et de termes italiens nouveaux selon la progression logique rencontrée dans une méthode de flûte à bec pour débutant. La démarche consiste à fournir des airs et des structures propres au répertoire de la flûte à bec de préférence à de stériles exercices de déchiffrage. Chaque partie débute par plusieurs pièces en solo et se termine par des duos et des pièces accompagnées de manière à familiariser l'instrumentiste avec le déchiffrage collectif.

Les cinq premières parties de cet ouvrage sont consacrées à la flûte à bec soprano. La flûte à bec alto est introduite dans la 6ème partie.

1ère partie. Notes *sol – si* sur des rythmes et des mesures simples. Les mélodies présentent des progressions par degrés conjoints, des structures de phrases simples, des notes répétées et des motifs mélodiques répétés (séquences).

2ème partie. Introduction des notes *do* et *ré* dans des mesures à 3/4, de mouvements mélodiques disjoints et de quelques suggestions de liaisons de phrasé.

3ème partie. Introduction du *fa♯* grave et du *do♯* aigu ainsi que de la tonalité de *ré* majeur et de son armure, de l'intervalle de quarte, de croches liées et du rythme noire pointée–croche (♩. ♪). Initiation à la notion de nuances avec f (fort) et p (doux).

4ème partie. Extension de la tessiture de *mi* et *ré* graves à *mi* aigu. Introduction de la mesure à 3/8 en préparation à la mesure à 6/8, de doubles croches par paires dans la mesure à 3/8 et de l'intervalle de quinte.

5ème partie. Extension de la tessiture du *do* grave au *fa♯* aigu et ajout de la tonalité de *ré* mineur. Valeurs rythmiques et mesures familières avec addition d'exemples à 5/4 et de trilles sous forme longue et courte.

6ème partie. Addition des notes *si♭*, *mi♭* et *la♭* et des tonalités de *fa* majeur et de *si♭* majeur. Introduction des tonalités de *do* mineur, *mi* mineur, *sol* mineur (alto) et *la* mineur ainsi que de l'intervalle de sixte. Ajout du mordant aux ornements déjà rencontrés et de brefs passages chromatiques. Initiation à la flûte à bec alto.

7ème partie. Introduction du *sol* aigu et des tonalités de *mi♭* majeur, de *mi* majeur (alto), et de *la* majeur. Passages chromatiques plus étendus. Recours au mordant inférieur et à des syncopes simples.

A l'élève : Pourquoi le déchiffrage ?

Lorsque vous vous trouvez face à un nouveau morceau que l'on vous demande de jouer, que ce soit chez vous, pendant une leçon ou lors d'un examen ou d'une audition, personne d'autre ne peut vous aider que vous-même ! Le déchiffrage met à l'épreuve votre capacité à lire correctement les rythmes et les notes et à saisir rapidement le phrasé et les nuances.

Ce recueil se propose de vous aider à vous entraîner vous-même. Il vous oriente sur ce que vous devez repérer et sur la meilleure manière de vous préparer en un laps de temps très court en sachant observer les indications de mesure et l'armure à la clef de la tonalité, les contours de la mélodie et les indications expressives. Ces pièces brèves, en progressant par étapes, vous feront prendre de l'assurance, aiguiseront vos observations et vous permettront de lire à vue avec exactitude et aisance. A la fin de chaque section figurent des duos que vous pourrez jouer avec votre professeur ou des amis et des morceaux avec accompagnement de piano qui mettront à l'épreuve votre habileté à déchiffrer pendant que se déroule une autre partie. Celle-ci est indispensable pour jouer dans un groupe, un orchestre ou un ensemble.

Vous serez surpris de vos progrès si vous déchiffrez une pièce à chaque fois que vous vous mettez à la flûte à bec. N'oubliez pas que si vous êtes capable de lire à vue la plupart des morceaux que vous allez étudier, vous pourrez vous concentrer sur les passages difficiles et les assimiler plus vite.

Considérez ces pages comme des « mini-morceaux » et essayez de les apprendre rapidement et sans erreur de manière à ce que, devant un véritable déchiffrage, vous soyez bien armé pour réussir dès la première lecture.

A vous seul de jouer maintenant !

Vorwort

Vom-Blatt-Spiel auf der Blockflöte 1 möchte zu einer guten Übepraxis verhelfen und frühzeitig für die Einführung der grundlegenden Fähigkeit des Blatt-Spiels sorgen.

Vom-Blatt-Spiel alleine zu üben hat wenig Sinn, wenn das Ergebnis nicht vom Lehrer überprüft wird. Idealerweise sollte das Vom-Blatt-Spiel in irgendeiner Form ein regelmäßiger Bestandteil des Übens werden.

Dieser Band hat zum Ziel, bereits von Anfang an diese Gewohnheit in das Blockflötenspiel des Schülers zu verankern. Natürlich muss man die Notennamen und Notenwerte komplett kennen und verstanden haben, aber durch das Bewusstsein für Form und Richtung wird das Vom-Blatt-Spiel gleichermaßen unterstützt.

Der Band hat sieben Teile, die nach und nach neue Noten, Rhythmen, Artikulation, Dynamik und italienische Begriffe in einer logischen Abfolge einführen – ganz ähnlich, wie man es in einer Blockflötenschule für Anfänger auch finden würde. Der Schwerpunkt liegt auf dem Bereitstellen passender Melodien und Strukturen anstelle von sterilen Vom-Blatt-Spiel Übungen. Jeder Teil beginnt mit einigen Solobeispielen und endet mit Duetten und begleiteten Stücken, damit man auch beim Zusammenspiel mit Anderen Erfahrungen mit dem Blattspiel sammeln kann.

Die Teile 1 bis 5 beschäftigen sich nur mit der Sopran-Blockflöte. Die Alt-Blockflöte wird in Teil 6 hinzugenommen.

Teil 1 benutzt die Töne g^2 – h^2 zusammen mit einfachen Rhythmen und Taktarten. Das melodische Material beschäftigt sich mit schrittweiser Bewegung, einfach strukturierten Phrasen sowie sich wiederholenden Noten und melodischen Formen (Sequenzen).

Teil 2 führt die Noten c^2 und d^2 sowie den 3/4-Takt ein. Sprünge kommen hinzu und einige Bindungen werden vorgeschlagen.

Teil 3 führt fis^2 und cis^3 zusammen mit der Tonart und den Vorzeichen von D-Dur ein. Sowohl die Quarte als auch einige gebundene Achtel kommen vor sowie die punktierte Viertel-Achtel-Figur (♩. ♪). Das dynamische Konzept wird vorgestellt, wobei *f* als ‚stark‘ und *p* als ‚sanft‘ interpretiert wird.

Teil 4 erweitert den Tonraum von d^2 bis d^3. Der 3/8-Takt wird eingeführt und mündet im Gebrauch des 6/8-Taktes. Sechzehntelnoten kommen paarweise im 3/8-Takt vor, und die Quinte wird vorgestellt.

Teil 5 erweitert den Tonumfang, vom c^2 bis zum fis^3 und führt die Tonart d-Moll ein. Bekannte Notenwerte und Taktarten werden benutzt, es gibt aber auch Beispiele für den 5/4-Takt. Sowohl lange als auch kurze Triller werden benutzt.

Teil 6 beschäftigt sich mit den Noten es^2 und es^3, as^2 und b^2 sowie den Tonarten F- und B-Dur. Die Tonarten c-, e-, g- (Alt-Blockflöte) und a-Moll sowie die Sexte werden ebenfalls eingeführt. Zu den bereits benutzten Verzierungen wird der Mordent hinzugefügt, und kurze chromatische Phrasen werden benutzt. Die Alt-Blockflöte wird vorgestellt.

Teil 7 führt das g^3 sowie die Tonarten Es-, E- und A-Dur ein. Ausgedehnte chromatische Phrasen, der Pralltriller und einige einfache Synkopen kommen zur Anwendung.

An den Schüler: Warum Vom-Blatt-Spiel?

Wenn du dich einem neuen Musikstück gegenüber siehst und gebeten wirst, es zu spielen, egal, ob zu Hause, im Unterricht, in einem Examen oder einem Vorspiel, gibt es niemanden, der dir helfen kann – nur du selbst! Das Blatt-Spiel testet die Fähigkeit, die Taktart und die Noten richtig zu lesen sowie Phrasierungen und Dynamik schnell zu erfassen.

Ziel dieser Ausgabe ist es, dir beim Selbstunterricht behilflich zu sein. Sie zeigt dir, worauf du achten sollst und wie du dich in sehr kurzer Zeit am besten vorbereitest. Das tust du, indem du dir Takt- und Tonart sowie den Verlauf der Melodie und die Ausdruckszeichen genau anschaust. Die kurzen Musikstücke steigern sich nur allmählich, um sowohl dein Vertrauen und deine Beobachtungsgabe aufzubauen als auch, um dich dazu zu befähigen, exakt vom Blatt zu spielen. Am Ende jeden Teils stehen Duette, die du mit deinem Lehrer oder deinen Freunden spielen kannst. Außerdem gibt es Stücke mit Klavierbegleitung, die deine Fähigkeit im Blatt-Spiel überprüfen, während gleichzeitig etwas anderes abläuft. Das ist eine wesentliche Fähigkeit, wenn man mit einer Band, einem Orchester oder einer anderen Musikgruppe zusammenspielt.

Wenn du jedes Mal, wenn du Blockflöte spielst, auch etwas vom Blatt spielst, wirst du überrascht sein, wie sehr du dich verbesserst. Denke daran: wenn du die meisten Melodien, die du spielen sollst, vom Blatt spielen kannst, kannst du dich auf die ‚schwierigen Teile‘ konzentrieren und diese viel schneller beherrschen.

Stelle dir die Melodien in diesem Band als ‚Ministücke‘ vor und versuche, sie schnell und korrekt zu lernen. Wenn du dann wirklich vom Blatt spielen musst, wirst du bestens ausgerüstet sein, um gleich beim ersten Versuch erfolgreich zu sein.

Jetzt bist du auf dich selbst gestellt!

Section 1 – Notes G, A and B
1ère partie – Notes *sol*, *la* et *si*
Teil 1 – Die Noten *g²*, *a²* und *h²*

Three steps to success

1. **Look at the top number of the time signature.** It shows the number of beats in the bar. Tap (clap, sing or play on one note) the rhythm, feeling the pulse throughout. Count at least one bar of the time signature in your head to set up the pulse before you tap or play the tune.

2. **Look for patterns.** While tapping the rhythm, look at the melodic shape and notice movement by step, repeated notes and sequences (short phrases that are repeated at higher or lower notes, often rising or falling by step).

3. **Keep going!** Remember, a wrong note or rhythm can be corrected the next time you play it. If you stop, you have doubled the mistake!

Trois étapes vers la réussite

1. **Observez le chiffre supérieur de l'indication de mesure.** Il indique le nombre de pulsations contenues par mesure. Frappez (dans les mains, chantez ou jouez sur une seule note) le rythme tout en maintenant une pulsation intérieure constante. Comptez mentalement au moins une mesure complète pour installer la pulsation avant de frapper ou de jouer chaque pièce.

2. **Repérez les motifs.** Tout en frappant le rythme, observez les contours de la mélodie et relevez les mouvements par degrés, les sauts d'intervalles, les notes répétées et les séquences (phrases brèves reprises sur des degrés plus aigus ou plus graves, procédant habituellement par mouvement ascendant ou descendant).

3. **Ne vous arrêtez pas !** Vous pourrez corriger une fausse note ou un rythme inexact la prochaine fois que vous jouerez. En vous interrompant, vous doublez la faute !

Drei Schritte zum Erfolg

1. **Schaue dir die obere Zahl der Taktangabe an.** Diese zeigt die Anzahl der Schläge in einem Takt. Schlage (klatsche, singe oder spiele auf einer Note) den Rhythmus, wobei du immer das Metrum spürst. Zähle mindestens einen Takt lang die Taktangabe im Kopf, um das Metrum zu verinnerlichen, bevor du jede der Melodien klopfst oder spielst.

2. **Achte auf Muster.** Schaue dir die melodische Form an, während du den Rhythmus schlägst und achte auf Bewegungen in Schritten oder Sprüngen, sich wiederholende Noten oder Sequenzen (kurze Phrasen, die auf höheren oder tieferen Noten wiederholt werden, wobei sie oft schrittweise ansteigen oder fallen).

3. **Bleibe dran!** Denke daran: eine falsche Note oder ein falscher Rhythmus kann beim nächsten Mal korrigiert werden. Wenn du aber aufhörst zu spielen, verdoppelst du den Fehler!

Section 1 – Notes G, A and B
1ère partie – Notes *sol, la* et *si*
Teil 1 – Die Noten g², a² und h²

10

20.

21.

22.

23.

24.

25.

26.

Section 2 – Notes G – D and slurs
2ᵉᵐᵉ partie – Notes *sol – ré* et liaisons de phrasé
Teil 2 – Die Noten g² – d³ und Bindungen

Four steps to success

1. **Look at the top number of the time signature.** It shows the number of beats in the bar. Tap (clap, sing or play on one note) the rhythm, feeling the pulse throughout. Count at least one bar of the time signature in your head to set up the pulse before you tap or play the tune.

2. **Look for patterns.** While tapping the rhythm, look at the melodic shape and notice movement by step, skips, repeated notes or sequences.

3. **Notice the slurring.** Often slurring is very logical. Similar phrases will usually have the same articulation.

4 Keep going!

Quatre étapes vers la réussite

1. **Observez le chiffre supérieur de l'indication de mesure.** Il indique le nombre de pulsations contenues par mesure. Frappez (dans les mains, chantez ou jouez sur une seule note) le rythme tout en maintenant une pulsation intérieure constante. Comptez mentalement au moins une mesure pour installer la pulsation avant de frappez ou de jouer chaque pièce.

2. **Repérez les motifs.** Tout en frappant le rythme, observez les contours de la mélodie et relevez les mouvements par degrés, les sauts d'intervalles, les notes répétées ou les séquences.

3. **Observez les liaisons de phrasé.** Celles-ci sont souvent très logiques, les phrases similaires étant en général phrasées de la même façon.

4. **Ne vous arrêtez pas !**

Vier Schritte zum Erfolg

1. **Schaue dir die obere Zahl der Taktangabe an.** Diese zeigt die Anzahl der Schläge in einem Takt. Schlage (klatsche, singe oder spiele auf einer Note) den Rhythmus, wobei du immer das Metrum spürst. Zähle mindestens einen Takt lang die Taktangabe im Kopf, um das Metrum zu verinnerlichen, bevor du jede der Melodien klopfst oder spielst.

2. **Achte auf Muster.** Schaue dir die melodische Form an, während du den Rhythmus schlägst und achte auf Bewegungen in Schritten oder Sprüngen, sich wiederholende Noten und Sequenzen.

3. **Konzentriere dich auf die Bindungen.** Bindungen sind oft sehr logisch. Ähnliche Phrasen haben normalerweise auch dieselbe Artikulation.

4. **Bleibe dran!**

14

Section 2 – Notes G – D and slurs

2ème partie – Notes *sol – ré* et liaisons de phrasé

Teil 2 – Die Noten g² – d³ und Bindungen

G major in 4/4 time.　　　　*sol* majeur dans une mesure　　　　G-Dur im 4/4-Takt.
　　　　　　　　　　　　　　　à 4 temps.

C major in 4/4 time.　　　　*do* majeur dans une mesure　　　　C-Dur im 4/4-Takt.
　　　　　　　　　　　　　　　à 4 temps.

G major in 2/4 time.   *sol* majeur dans une mesure   G-Dur im 2/4-Takt.
                                        à 2 temps.

33.

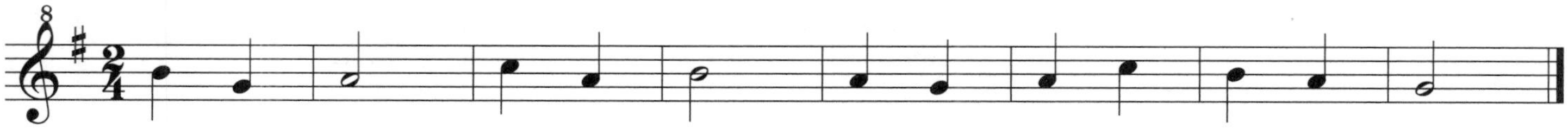

C major in 2/4 time.   *do* majeur dans une mesure   C-Dur im 2/4-Takt.
                                        à 2 temps.

34.

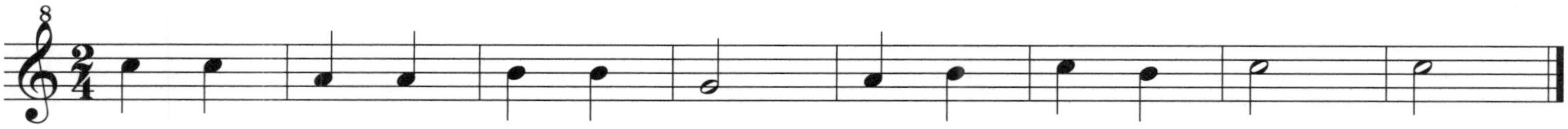

3/4 time.   Mesure à 3/4.   3/4-Takt.

35.

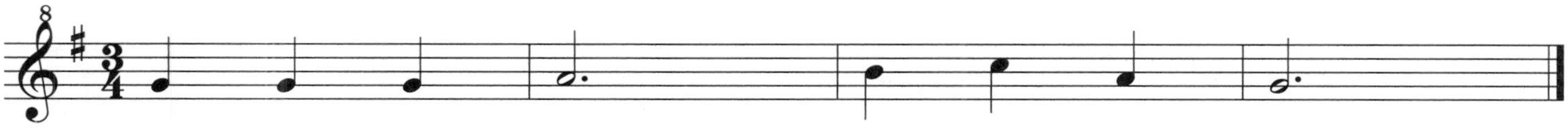

36.

C major.   *do* majeur.   C-Dur.

37.

38.

Longer pieces in 2-, 3- and 4-time.   Pièces plus longues à 2, 3 et 4   Längere Stücke im 2/4-, 3/4- und
                                        temps.   4/4-Takt.

39.

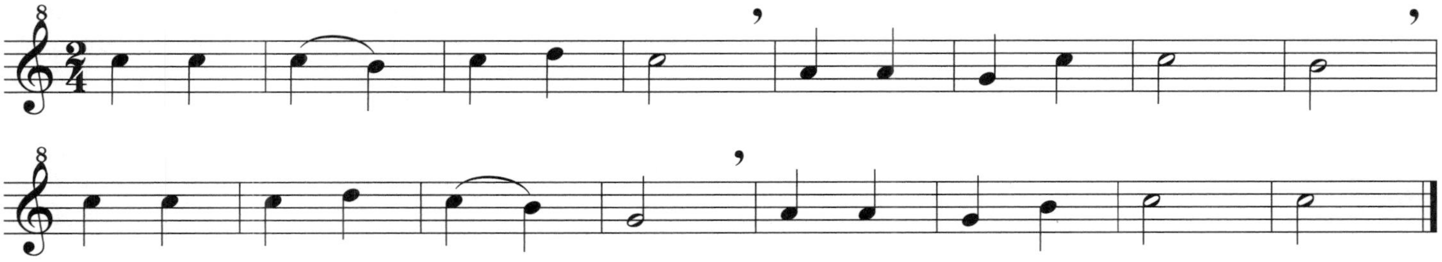

40.

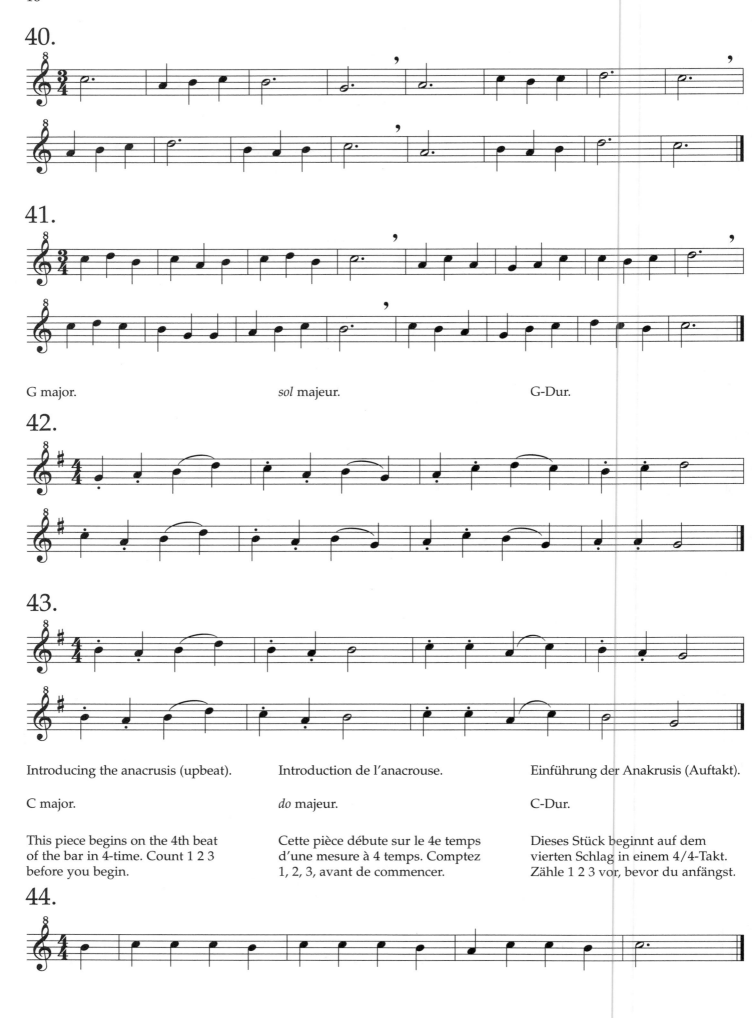

41.

G major.   *sol* majeur.   G-Dur.

42.

43.

Introducing the anacrusis (upbeat).   Introduction de l'anacrouse.   Einführung der Anakrusis (Auftakt).

C major.   *do* majeur.   C-Dur.

This piece begins on the 4th beat of the bar in 4-time. Count 1 2 3 before you begin.   Cette pièce débute sur le 4e temps d'une mesure à 4 temps. Comptez 1, 2, 3, avant de commencer.   Dieses Stück beginnt auf dem vierten Schlag in einem 4/4-Takt. Zähle 1 2 3 vor, bevor du anfängst.

44.

This piece begins on the 3rd beat of the bar in 3-time. Count 1 2 3 1 2 before you begin.

Cette pièce débute sur le 3e temps d'une mesure à 3 temps. Comptez 1, 2, 3, 1, 2, avant de commencer.

Dieses Stück beginnt auf dem dritten Schlag in einem 3/4-Takt. Zähle 1 2 3 1 2 vor, bevor du anfängst.

45.

This piece begins on the 2nd beat of the bar in 2-time. Count 1 2 1 before you begin.

Cette pièce débute sur le 2e temps d'une mesure à 2 temps. Comptez 1, 2, 1, avant de commencer.

Dieses Stück beginnt auf dem zweiten Schlag in einem 2/4-Takt. Zähle 1 2 1 vor, bevor du anfängst.

46.

G major.

sol majeur.

G-Dur.

This piece begins on the 4th beat of the bar in 4-time. Count 1 2 3 before you begin.

Cette pièce débute sur le 4e temps d'une mesure à 4 temps. Comptez 1, 2, 3, avant de commencer.

Dieses Stück beginnt auf dem vierten Schlag in einem 4/4-Takt. Zähle 1 2 3 vor, bevor du anfängst.

47.

This piece begins on the 3rd beat of the bar in 3-time. Count 1 2 3 1 2 before you begin.

Cette pièce débute sur le 3e temps d'une mesure à 3 temps. Comptez 1, 2, 3, 1, 2, avant de commencer.

Dieses Stück beginnt auf dem dritten Schlag in einem 3/4-Takt. Zähle 1 2 3 1 2 vor, bevor du anfängst.

48.

This piece begins on the 2nd beat of the bar in 2-time. Count 1 2 1 before you begin.

Cette pièce débute sur le 2e temps d'une mesure à 2 temps. Comptez 1, 2, 1, avant de commencer.

Dieses Stück beginnt auf dem zweiten Schlag in einem 2/4-Takt. Zähle 1 2 1 vor, bevor du anfängst.

49.

18

This piece begins on the 4th beat
of the bar in 4-time. Count 1 2 3
before you begin.

Cette pièce débute sur le 4e temps
d'une mesure à 4 temps. Comptez
1, 2, 3, avant de commencer.

Dieses Stück beginnt auf dem
vierten Schlag in einem 4/4-Takt.
Zähle 1 2 3 vor, bevor du anfängst.

50.

Pupil/Elève/Schüler

Teacher/Professeur/Lehrer

51.

52.

This piece begins on the 4th beat
of the bar in 4-time. Count 1 2 3
before you begin.

Cette pièce débute sur le 4e temps
d'une mesure à 4 temps. Comptez
1, 2, 3, avant de commencer.

Dieses Stück beginnt auf dem
vierten Schlag in einem 4/4-Takt.
Zähle 1 2 3 vor, bevor du anfängst.

53.

54.

55.

56.

57.

21

58.

Section 3 – Notes low F♯ and high C♯; ♩. ♪ rhythm and performance directions

3ᵉᵐᵉ partie – Notes *fa*♯ grave et *do*♯ aigu ; rythme ♩. ♪ et indications d'exécution

Teil 3 – Die Noten fis² und cis³; ♩. ♪-Rhythmus und Vortragsangaben

Five steps to success

1. **Look at the top number of the time signature.** It shows the number of beats in a bar. Tap (clap, sing or play on one note) the rhythm, feeling the pulse throughout. Count at least one bar of the time signature in your head to set up the pulse before you tap or play each tune.

2. **Look between the treble clef and the time signature for any sharps or flats.** This is known as the key signature. Make sure you know which notes the sharps or flats apply to and notice where they occur in the melody.

3. **Look for patterns.** While tapping the rhythm, look at the melodic shape and notice movement by step, skips, repeated notes or sequences.

4. **Notice the articulation and dynamics.** Observe the dynamic shapes and notice if they change suddenly or gradually.

5. **Keep going!**

Cinq étapes vers la réussite

1. **Observez le chiffre supérieur de l'indication de mesure.** Il indique le nombre de pulsations contenues par mesure. Frappez (dans les mains, chantez ou jouez sur une seule note) le rythme tout en maintenant une pulsation intérieure constante. Comptez mentalement au moins une mesure pour installer la pulsation avant de frapper ou de jouer chaque pièce.

2. **Vérifiez les dièses ou les bémols placés entre la clef de sol et les chiffres indicateurs de mesure.** Ceux-ci constituent l'armure de la tonalité. Assurez-vous des notes altérées et repérez-les dans la mélodie.

3. **Repérez les motifs.** Tout en frappant le rythme, observez les contours de la mélodie et relevez les déplacements par degrés, les sauts d'intervalles, les notes répétées et les séquences.

4. **Observez le phrasé et les nuances.** Notez les nuances dynamiques et leurs changements subits ou progressifs.

5. **Ne vous arrêtez pas !**

Fünf Schritte zum Erfolg

1. **Schaue dir die obere Zahl der Taktangabe an.** Schlage (klatsche, singe oder spiele auf einer Note) den Rhythmus, wobei du immer das Metrum spürst. Zähle mindestens einen Takt lang die Taktangabe im Kopf, um das Metrum zu verinnerlichen, bevor du jede der Melodien klopfst oder spielst.

2. **Achte auf Kreuz- und B-Vorzeichen zwischen dem Notenschlüssel und der Taktangabe.** Diese ergeben die Tonart. Vergewissere dich, dass du weißt, auf welche Noten sie sich beziehen und wo sie in der Melodie auftauchen.

3. **Achte auf Muster.** Schaue dir die melodische Form an, während du den Rhythmus schlägst und achte auf Bewegungen in Schritten oder Sprüngen, sich wiederholende Noten und Sequenzen.

4. **Beachte Bindungen und Dynamik.** Schaue dir die dynamischen Formen genau an und registriere, ob sich die dynamischen Formen plötzlich oder allmählich ändern.

5. **Bleibe dran!**

Performance directions used in this section (you may note all directions and translations on the glossary page at the back of the book):

Indications d'exécution utilisées dans cette partie (vous pourrez noter toutes les indications et leur traduction sur la page de glossaire en fin de volume) :

Vortragsangaben, die in diesem Teil verwendet werden (du kannst alle Angaben und Übersetzungen in der Anhangseite am Ende aufschreiben):

Alla marcia	in the style of a march	en style de marche	marschmäßig
Allegretto	not as fast as Allegro	moins rapide qu'*allegro*	nicht so schnell wie Allegro
Allegro	fast	rapide	schnell
Allegro moderato	moderately fast	modérément rapide	gemäßigt schnell
Andante	at a walking pace	allant	gehend
Andante moderato	at a moderate walking pace	modérément allant	in gemäßigtem Tempo
Con moto	with movement	avec mouvement	mit Bewegung
Gavotte	a lively dance beginning on the 3rd beat in 4-time	danse vive commençant sur le 3ème temps d'une mesure à 4 temps	ein lebhafter Tanz, der auf dem dritten Schlag in einem 4/4-Takt beginnt
Maestoso	majestic	majestueusement	majestätisch
Moderato	at a moderate speed	modéré	gemäßigt
Ritmico	rhythmical	rythmé	rhythmisch
Spiritoso	spirited	avec esprit	geistreich
Vivace	lively	vif	lebhaft
Waltz	a dance in 3-time	danse à trois temps	ein Tanz im 3er-Takt
	Dynamics	**Nuances**	**Dynamik**
$\boldsymbol{f}$ (forte)	loud (strong)	fort	laut (kräftig)
$\boldsymbol{p}$ (piano)	soft (gentle)	doux	leise (sanft)

Section 3 – Notes low F♯ and high C♯; ♩. ♪ rhythm and performance directions

3ème partie – Notes *fa*♯ grave et *do*♯ aigu ; rythme ♩. ♪ et indications d'exécution

Teil 3 – Die Noten fis² und cis³; ♩. ♪-Rhythmus und Vortragsangaben

G major.   *sol* majeur.   G-Dur.

C major.   *do* majeur.   C-Dur.

G major.   *sol* majeur.   G-Dur.

63.

D major.   *ré* majeur.   D-Dur.

64.

65.

66.

Adding quavers (eighth notes).   Introduction des croches.   Einführung von Achteln.

G major.   *sol* majeur.   G-Dur.

67.

C major.   *do* majeur.   C-Dur.

68.

D major.   *ré* majeur.   D-Dur.

69.

G major.   *sol* majeur.   G-Dur.

70.

The anacrusis (upbeat).

This piece begins on the 4th beat of the bar in 4-time. Count 1 2 3 before you begin.

L'anacrouse.

Cette pièce débute sur le 4e temps d'une mesure à 4 temps. Comptez 1, 2, 3, avant de commencer.

Die Anakrusis (Auftakt).

Dieses Stück beginnt auf dem vierten Schlag in einem 4/4-Takt. Zähle 1 2 3 vor, bevor du anfängst.

71.

This piece begins on the 3rd beat of the bar in 3-time. Count 1 2 3 1 2 before you begin.

Cette pièce débute sur le 3e temps d'une mesure à 3 temps. Comptez 1, 2, 3, 1, 2, avant de commencer.

Dieses Stück beginnt auf dem dritten Schlag in einem 3/4-Takt. Zähle 1 2 3 1 2 vor, bevor du anfängst.

72.

This piece begins on the 4th beat of the bar in 4-time. Count 1 2 3 before you begin.

Cette pièce débute sur le 4e temps d'une mesure à 4 temps. Comptez 1, 2, 3, avant de commencer.

Dieses Stück beginnt auf dem vierten Schlag in einem 4/4-Takt. Zähle 1 2 3 vor, bevor du anfängst.

73.

This piece begins on the 3rd beat of the bar in 3-time. Count 1 2 3 1 2 before you begin.

Cette pièce débute sur le 3e temps d'une mesure à 3 temps. Comptez 1, 2, 3, 1, 2, avant de commencer.

Dieses Stück beginnt auf dem dritten Schlag in einem 3/4-Takt. Zähle 1 2 3 1 2 vor, bevor du anfängst.

74.

This piece begins on the 2nd beat of the bar in 2-time. Count 1 2 1 before you begin.

Cette pièce débute sur le 2e temps d'une mesure à 2 temps. Comptez 1, 2, 1, avant de commencer.

Dieses Stück beginnt auf dem zweiten Schlag in einem 2/4-Takt. Zähle 1 2 1 vor, bevor du anfängst.

75.

Introducing 𝅗𝅥. ♪

Introduction du rythme 𝅗𝅥. ♪

Einführung von 𝅗𝅥. ♪

76.

77.

28

This piece begins on the 4th beat of the bar in 4-time. Count 1 2 3 before you begin.

Cette pièce débute sur le 4e temps d'une mesure à 4 temps. Comptez 1, 2, 3, avant de commencer.

Dieses Stück beginnt auf dem vierten Schlag in einem 4/4-Takt. Zähle 1 2 3 vor, bevor du anfängst.

78.

Andante

This piece begins on the 3rd beat of the bar in 3-time. Count 1 2 3 1 2 before you begin.

Cette pièce débute sur le 3e temps d'une mesure à 3 temps. Comptez 1, 2, 3, 1, 2, avant de commencer.

Dieses Stück beginnt auf dem dritten Schlag in einem 3/4-Takt. Zähle 1 2 3 1 2 vor, bevor du anfängst.

79.

Con moto

This piece begins on the 4th beat of the bar in 4-time. Count 1 2 3 before you begin.

Cette pièce débute sur le 4e temps d'une mesure à 4 temps. Comptez 1, 2, 3, avant de commencer.

Dieses Stück beginnt auf dem vierten Schlag in einem 4/4-Takt. Zähle 1 2 3 vor, bevor du anfängst.

80.

Allegretto

81.

Moderato

82.

Allegro

83.

This piece begins on the 3rd beat of the bar in 3-time. Count 1 2 3 1 2 before you begin.

Cette pièce débute sur le 3e temps d'une mesure à 3 temps. Comptez 1, 2, 3, 1, 2, avant de commencer.

Dieses Stück beginnt auf dem dritten Schlag in einem 3/4-Takt. Zähle 1 2 3 1 2 vor, bevor du anfängst.

84.

85.

86.

This piece begins on the 4th beat of the bar in 4-time. Count 1 2 3 before you begin.

Cette pièce débute sur le 4e temps d'une mesure à 4 temps. Comptez 1, 2, 3, avant de commencer.

Dieses Stück beginnt auf dem vierten Schlag in einem 4/4-Takt. Zähle 1 2 3 vor, bevor du anfängst.

87.

This piece begins on the 4th beat of the bar in 4-time. Count 1 2 3 before you begin.

Cette pièce débute sur le 4e temps d'une mesure à 4 temps. Comptez 1, 2, 3, avant de commencer.

Dieses Stück beginnt auf dem vierten Schlag in einem 4/4-Takt. Zähle 1 2 3 vor, bevor du anfängst.

88.

89.

Andante moderato

90.

Gavotte

91.

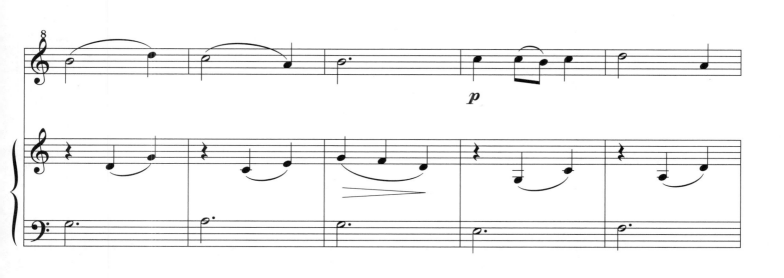

92.

93.

Section 4 – Notes low D to high E; 3/8 and 6/8

4ᵉᵐᵉ partie – Notes *ré* grave à *mi* aigu ; mesures à 3/8 et 6/8

Teil 4 – Die Noten d² bis e³; der 3/8- und 6/8-Takt

Follow the **steps to success**

Follow the steps of the last section:

1. Look at the top number of the time signature. You now need also to start looking at the bottom number. There are some new time signatures included in this section. Follow the exercises described in the previous section to ensure that you get a sense of the pulse.

2, 3 and 4. Look for sharps and flats, for patterns, and for articulations and dynamics.

Suivez les **étapes vers la réussite**

Suivez les étapes de la partie précédente :

1. Observez le chiffre supérieur de l'indication de mesure. Commencez également à vous intéresser au chiffre inférieur. Cette partie présente de nouvelles indications de mesure. Reprenez les exercices décrits dans la partie précédente pour consolider votre sens de la pulsation.

2, 3 et 4. Repérez les altérations, les motifs, les phrasés et les nuances.

Folge den **Schritten zum Erfolg**

Folge den Schritten des letzten Teils:

1. Schaue dir die obere Zahl der Taktangabe an. Beginne nun auch auf die untere Zahl zu achten. In diesem Teil kommen einige neue Taktangaben vor. Folge den Übungen (klatsche, singe oder spiele den Rhythmus) des letzten Teils, um ein Taktgefühl zu entwickeln.

2, 3 und 4. Achte auf Kreuz- und B-Vorzeichen, Muster, Artikulationen sowie dynamische Angaben.

Performance directions introduced in this section:

Indications d'exécution rencontrées dans cette partie :

Vortragsangaben, die in diesem Teil verwendet werden:

Adagio	slowly	lent	langsam
Alla giga	in the style of a gigue	en style de gigue	im Stile einer Gigue
Boldly (Italian: arditamente)	(boldly)	hardiment	in kühner Weise
Con brio	with life	avec éclat	mit Feuer
Minuet	a stately dance in 3-time	danse majesteuse à trois temps	ein Tanz im 3/4-Takt in mäßigem Tempo
Vivo	lively	vif, rapide	schnell/lebhaft
	Dynamics	**Nuances**	**Dynamik**
mf (mezzo forte)	moderately loud (normal)	moyennement fort	gemäßigt laut (normal)

Section 4 – Notes low D to high E; 3/8 and 6/8

4ème partie – Notes *ré* grave à *mi* aigu ; mesures à 3/8 et 6/8

Teil 4 – Die Noten d² bis e³; der 3/8- und 6/8-Takt

94.

This piece begins on the 3rd beat of the bar in 3-time. Count 1 2 3 1 2 before you begin.	Cette pièce débute sur le 3e temps d'une mesure à 3 temps. Comptez 1, 2, 3, 1, 2, avant de commencer.	Dieses Stück beginnt auf dem dritten Schlag in einem 3/4-Takt. Zähle 1 2 3 1 2 vor, bevor du anfängst.

95.

96.

97.

Minuet

This piece begins on the 3rd beat of the bar in 3-time. Count 1 2 3 1 2 before you begin.

Cette pièce débute sur le 3e temps d'une mesure à 3 temps. Comptez 1, 2, 3, 1, 2, avant de commencer.

Dieses Stück beginnt auf dem dritten Schlag in einem 3/4-Takt. Zähle 1 2 3 1 2 vor, bevor du anfängst.

98.

Andante

99.

Gavotte

Introducing 3/8 time.

Introduction des mesures à 3/8.

Einführung des 3/8-Takts.

100.

Moderato

This piece begins on the 3rd beat of the bar in 3-time. Count 1 2 3 1 2 before you begin.

Cette pièce débute sur le 3e temps d'une mesure à 3 temps. Comptez 1, 2, 3, 1, 2, avant de commencer.

Dieses Stück beginnt auf dem dritten Schlag in einem 3/4-Takt. Zähle 1 2 3 1 2 vor, bevor du anfängst.

101.

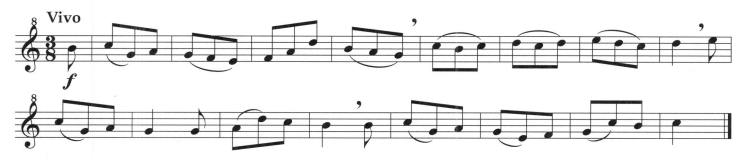

Introducing semiquavers (sixteenth notes).

Introduction des double croches.

Einführung von Achteln.

102.

103.

104.

105.

106.

Introducing 6/8 time.   Introduction des mesures à 6/8.   Einführung des 6/8-Takts.

107.

This piece begins on the last quaver in 6/8 time. Count two dotted crotchets in each bar. Count 1-2 1-2 before you begin.

Cette pièce commence sur la dernière croche d'une mesure à 6/8. Comptez deux noires pointées par mesure. Comptez mentalement 1, 2, 1, 2 avant d'attaquer.

Dieses Stück beginnt auf dem letzten Achtel in einem 6/8-Takt. Zähle zwei punktierte Viertel in jedem Takt. Zähle 1-2 1-2 bevor du anfängst.

108.

109.

This piece begins on the last quaver in 6/8 time. Count **1** (2 3) **2** (2) before you begin.

Cette pièce débute sur la dernière croche d'une mesure à 6/8. Comptez **1** (2, 3), **2** (2), avant de commencer.

Dieses Stück beginnt auf dem letzten Achtel in einem 6/8-Takt. Zähle **1** (2 3) **2** (2) bevor du anfängst.

110.

Adagio (in a modal style)

This piece begins on the last quaver in 6/8 time. Count 1-2 1-2 before you begin.

Cette pièce débute sur la dernière croche d'une mesure à 6/8. Comptez 1, 2, 1, 2 avant de commencer.

Dieses Stück beginnt auf dem letzten Achtel in einem 6/8-Takt. Zähle 1-2 1-2 bevor du anfängst.

111.

Vivace

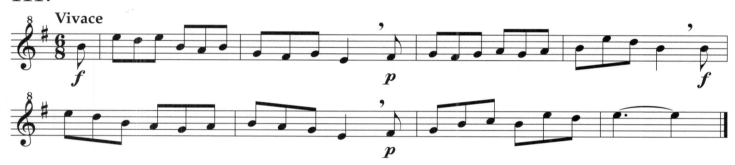

112.

Maestoso

113.

114.

115.

Both parts may be played by pupils.

Les deux parties peuvent être jouées par des élèves.

Beide Stimmen können von Schülern gespielt werden.

116.

117.

118.

119.

120.

Allegro moderato

121.

Section 5 – Notes low C to high F#; 5/4 and trills

5ème partie – Notes *do* grave à *fa*# aigu ; mesure à 5/4 et trilles

Teil 5 – Die Noten c² bis fis³; der 5/4-Takt und Triller

Follow the **steps to success** as before.

As well as the introduction of some new notes for a wider range, there is a new time signature in this section: 5/4.

Trills (alternating the written note with the note above a few times) are also used sometimes in the following pieces – they are shown by the symbol *tr* .

Suivez les mêmes **étapes vers la réussite** que précédemment.

Cette partie présente une nouvelle mesure à 5/4, à côté de nouvelles notes élargissant la tessiture.

Les trilles (alternance répétées de la note réelle et de la note supérieure) apparaissent plusieurs fois dans les pièces suivantes. Ils sont indiqués par le signe *tr* .

Folge wie bisher den **Schritten zum Erfolg.**

Neben einiger neuer Noten in einem größeren Tonumfang, wird auch der 5/4-Takt eingeführt.

Triller (sehr schnelle Bewegungen zwischen den geschriebenen und den darüberliegenden Noten) kommen in einigen der folgenden Stücken vor – schaue einfach nach dem Triller-Symbol *tr* .

Performance directions introduced in this section:

Indications d'exécution rencontrées dans cette partie :

Vortragsangaben, die in diesem Teil verwendet werden:

Andantino	a little quicker than Andante	un peu plus vite qu'*andante*	ein bisschen schneller als Andante
Cantabile	in a singing style	chantant	gesangvoll
Cresc., crescendo	gradually getting louder	de plus en plus fort	lauter werdend
Dolce	sweet	doux	süß
Espress., espressivo	expressive	expressif	ausdrucksvoll
Grazioso	graceful	gracieux	anmutig
Poco a poco	little by little	peu à peu	nach und nach
Risoluto	resolute	résolu	entschieden
Tempo comodo	at a convenient speed	au mouvement convenable	in einem angenehmen Tempo
Veloce	fast	rapide	rasch
	Dynamics	**Nuances**	**Dynamik**
mp (mezzo piano)	moderately soft	moyennement doux	halbleise (zwischen *p* und *mf*)
◁ (cresc.)	gradually getting louder	de plus en plus fort	allmählich lauter werdend
▷ (dim.)	gradually getting quieter	de plus en plus doux	allmählich leiser werdend

Section 5 – Notes low C to high F♯; 5/4 and trills
5ème partie – Notes *do* grave à *fa*♯ aigu ; mesure à 5/4 et trilles

Teil 5 – Die Noten c² bis fis³; der 5/4-Takt und Triller

122.

123.

124.

125.

126.

127.

128.

129.

130.

131.

132.

133.

134.

135.

138.

Allegretto

139.

Maestoso

p

poco a poco cresc.

f

140.

Grazioso

mf

141.

142.

143.

144.

145.

Section 6 – Notes high and low E♭/D♯, A♭/G♯ and B♭, chromatic phrases and the alto recorder

6ème partie – Notes *mi♭/ré♯* aigu et grave, *la♭/sol♯, si♭*, chromatismes et flûte à bec alto

Teil 6 – Die Noten es²/dis², es³/dis³, as²/gis² und b², chromatische Phrasen und Einführung der Alt-Blockflöte

Six steps to success

1. **Look at the time signature.**

2. **Look between the treble clef and the time signature for any sharps or flats.**

3. **Look out for accidentals.** Check that you know the fingering before you arrive at the note.

4. **Look for patterns.**

5. **Notice the articulation and dynamics.**

6. **Keep going!**

Six étapes vers la réussite

1. **Observez l'indication de mesure.**

2. **Vérifiez les dièses ou les bémols placés entre la clef de sol et l'indication de mesure.**

3. **Recherchez les altérations accidentelles.** Vérifiez votre doigté avant d'atteindre la note.

4. **Repérez les motifs.**

5. **Observez le phrasé et les nuances.**

6. **Ne vous arrêtez pas !**

Sechs Schritte zum Erfolg

1. **Schaue dir die obere Zahl der Taktangabe an.**

2. **Achte auf die Tonartenvorzeichen.**

3. **Suche nach Notenvorzeichen.** Stelle sicher, dass du die Greifweise kennst, bevor du diese Note erreichst.

4. **Achte auf Muster.**

5. **Beachte Artikulation und Dynamik.**

6. **Bleibe dran!**

Performance directions introduced in this section:

Indications d'exécution rencontrées dans cette partie :

Vortragsangaben, die in diesem Teil verwendet werden:

Canon	a piece where the parts imitate each other (e.g. 'London's Burning')	pièces dans laquelle les parties entrent en imitation	ein Musikstück, in dem ein Teil dem/den anderen imitierend nachfolgt – ganz ähnlich wie ein Rundtanz
Minuetto	minuet, a dance in 3-time	menuet, danse à 3 temps	ein Tanz im 3er-Takt
Poco adagio	a little slowly	un peu lent	ein wenig langsam

	Ornaments	**Ornements**	**Verzierungen**
	upper mordent, played as	mordant supérieur, s'exécute	der ‚obere' Mordent wird wie folgt gespielt:

	Play the note itself, the note above and back to the original note, as quickly as possible, but retaining clarity.	Jouez la note réelle, la note au-dessus d'elle et revenez à la note réelle aussi vite que possible mais avec clarté.	Spiele die Note selbst, dann die darüberliegende Note und wieder die Ausgangsnote so schnell wie möglich, aber ohne an Klarheit zu verlieren.

Section 6 – Notes high and low E♭/D♯, A♭/G♯ and B♭, chromatic phrases and the alto recorder

6ème partie – Notes *mi♭/ré♯* aigu et grave, *la♭/sol♯*, *si♭*, chromatismes et flûte à bec alto

Teil 6 – Die Noten es²/dis², es³/dis³, as²/gis² und b², chromatische Phrasen und Einführung der Alt-Blockflöte

146.

147.

62

148.

149.

150.

151.

152.

153.

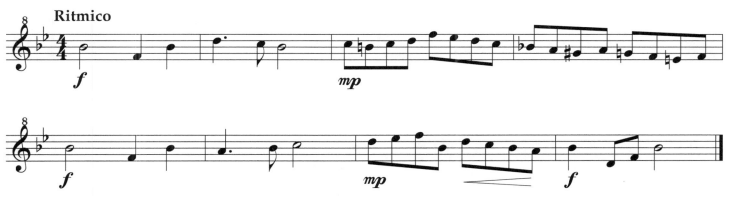

154.

155.

156.

Change-over (soprano – alto)

Note: the music for the soprano (descant) recorder sounds an octave higher than it is written. A little '8' is placed at the top of the clef to indicate this. A C major scale for the soprano recorder is written like this:

Echange de flûte (soprano – alto)

N.B. : la musique jouée à la flûte à bec soprano sonne à l'octave supérieure de sa notation. Un petit '8' est placée au-dessus de la clef pour signifier cet état de fait. La gamme de *do* majeur notée ainsi pour la flûte à bec soprano :

Umstellung (Sopran-Blockflöte – Alt-Blockflöte)

Anmerkung: die Noten der Sopran-Blockflöte klingen eine Oktave höher als sie geschrieben werden. Um das anzuzeigen, steht eine kleine ‚8' über dem Notenschlüssel. Eine C-Dur Tonleiter für die Sopran-Blockflöte kann wie folgt notiert werden:

but actually sounds at this pitch:

sonne en réalité à cette hauteur :

klingt aber tatsächlich in dieser Höhe:

The same scale for the alto recorder is written at the sounding pitch:

Pour la flûte à bec alto, la même gamme est notée à sa hauteur réelle :

Die gleiche Tonleiter für die Alt-Blockflöte wird in der tatsächlich klingenden Tonhöhe notiert:

Play the following tune, first on the soprano recorder:

Jouez le thème suivant, à la flûte à bec soprano :

Spiele die folgende Melodie, auf der Sopran-Blockflöte:

157a.

Range:
Etendue :
Tonumfang:

And then on the alto:

puis à la flûte à bec alto :

Und dann auf der Alt-Blockflöte:

157b.

Range:
Etendue :
Tonumfang:

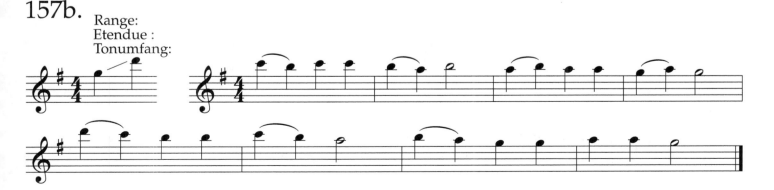

158a.

158b.

159a.

159b.

160a.

160b.

161.

162.

163.

164.

167.

168.

169.

Soprano.   Soprano.   Sopran-Blockflöte.

170.

171.

172.

Section 7 – Notes high G (soprano) and high D (alto)

7ème partie – Notes *sol* aigu (soprano) et *ré* aigu (alto)

Teil 7 – Die Noten g³ (Sopran-Blockflöte) und d³ (Alt-Blockflöte)

Six steps to success	Six étapes vers la réussite	Sechs Schritte zum Erfolg
1. Look at the time signature.	1. Observez l'indication de mesure.	1. Schaue dir die obere Zahl der Taktangabe an.
2. Look at the key signature.	2. Vérifiez les dièses ou les bémols placés entre la clef de sol et l'indication de mesure.	2. Achte auf die Tonartenvorzeichen.
3. Look out for accidentals.	3. Recherchez les altérations accidentelles.	3. Suche nach Notenvorzeichen.
4. Look for patterns.	4. Repérez les motifs.	4. Achte auf Muster.
5. Notice the articulation and dynamics.	5. Observez le phrasé et les nuances.	5. Beachte Artikulation und Dynamik.
6. Keep going!	6. Ne vous arrêtez pas !	6. Bleibe dran!

Performance directions introduced in this section: | *Indications d'exécution rencontrées dans cette partie :* | *Vortragsangaben, die in diesem Teil verwendet werden:*

A tempo	return to original tempo	au mouvement original	im ursprünglichen Tempo
Alla gavotta	in the style of a gavotte	en style de gavotte	im Stile einer Gavotte
Allegro ma non troppo	fast, but not too fast	rapide mais pas trop	schnell, aber nicht zu schnell
Dim. e rall.	gradually getting slower and quieter	de plus en plus doux et lent	allmählich leiser und langsamer werdend
Legato	smoothly	lié	gebunden
Leggiero	lightly	léger	leicht
Molto rit.	getting rapidly slower	en ralentissant beaucoup	viel langsamer werdend
Ragtime	a style of syncopated early jazz	style de jazz syncopé habituellement à 2 temps	ein früher Jazzstil mit vielen Synkopen, der normalerweise im 2er-Takt steht

Ornaments | **Ornements** | **Verzierungen**

lower mordent, played as: | le mordant inférieur, qui s'exécute : | der ‚untere' Mordent wird wie folgt gespielt:

Section 7 – Notes high G (soprano) and high D (alto)

7ᵉᵐᵉ partie – Notes *sol* aigu (soprano) et *ré* aigu (alto)

Teil 7 – Die Noten g³ (Sopran-Blockflöte) und d³ (Alt-Blockflöte)

Soprano.   Soprano.   Sopran-Blockflöte.

174.

175.

180.

Allegro

Alto.   Alto.   Alt-Blockflöte.

181.

Minuetto

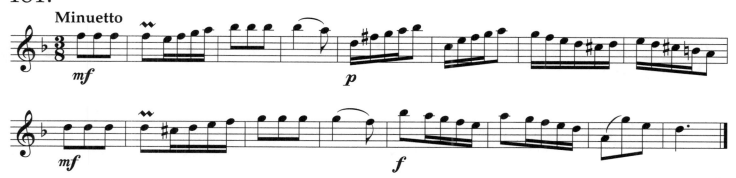

This piece begins on the 2nd beat in 3-time. Count 1 2 3 1 before you begin.

Cette pièce débute sur le 2e temps d'une mesure à 3 temps. Comptez 1, 2, 3, 1, avant de commencer.

Dieses Stück beginnt auf dem zweiten Schlag in einem 3/4-Takt. Zähle 1 2 3 1 vor, bevor du anfängst.

182.

Vivace

183.

184.

185.

189.

190.

191.

192.

82

193.

194.

Soprano. Soprano. Sopran-Blockflöte.

195.

196.

197.

198.

Alto. Alto. Alt-Blockflöte.

199.

200.

Glossary
Glossaire
Glossar

Note performance directions used throughout the book together with their translations so that you have a complete list. Writing them down will help you to remember them.

Inscrivez ici les indications d'exécution utilisées dans ce volume et leur traduction pour en établir une liste complète. Le fait de les noter vous aidera à les retenir.

Schreibe hier alle Vortragszeichen, die in diesem Band verwendet werden, zusammen mit ihrer Übersetzung auf, so dass du eine vollständige Liste hast. Das Aufschreiben wird dir dabei helfen, sie dir einzuprägen.

Adagio	Slowly	Lent	Langsam

Fun and Games with the Recorder
A special method for beginners

Fun and Games with the Recorder is a comprehensive recorder tutor ranging from the beginner's first notes to advanced playing.

- Discover the adventure of learning the recorder

- Make real progress through games: breathing, articulation, rhythm and tone

- Enjoy a mixture of lively new and traditional tunes

- Join Dotty-do-a-lot and her friends in the exciting world of music!

NEW: *Ensemble Collection* (ED 12911)

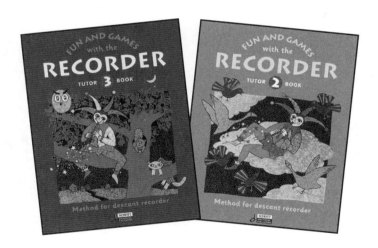

Descant (Soprano) Recorder

Tutor Book 1	(ED 12590)
Tutor Book 2	(ED 12592)
Tutor Book 3	(ED 12594)
Tune Book 1	(ED 12591)
Tune Book 2	(ED 12593)
Tune Book 3	(ED 12595)
Teacher's Commentary	(ED 12596)

Treble (Alto) Recorder

Tutor Book 1	(ED 12703)
Tutor Book 2	(ED 12705)
Tune Book 1	(ED 12704)
Tune Book 2	(ED 12706)
Teacher's Commentary	(ED 12707)

Also available: ***Fun and Games with the Recorder at Christmas*** (ED 12910)

SCHOTT

www.schott-music.com